Naughty Words for Nice Writers

A Romance Novel Thesaurus

Third Edition

Cara Bristol

To Mr. Durazo, my seventh grade English teacher,
who introduced us to the thesaurus.
We would have liked one with dirty words.

Naughty Words for Nice Writers, A Romance Novel Thesaurus
Copyright © March 2015 by Cara Bristol
Copyright © February 2017 by Cara Bristol
Revised January 2021

ISBN: 978-0-9908052-7-4
Editor: Kate Richards
Cover Artist: Sweet 'N Spicy Designs,
http://sweetnspicydesigns.com

Published in the United States of America

Cara Bristol

http://www.carabristol.com

Table of Contents

Introduction: Why a Sex Scene Thesaurus

When I started writing erotic romance in 2009, the first thing that struck me was the lack of positive romantic synonyms for the sex act in the English language. A standard thesaurus offered few entries with the vocabulary needed to write sex scenes.

Other than "making love" (positive) or having sex (neutral), sexual terms are clinical, crude, or ribald, none of which foster the intimacy one strives for in a romance. By default, writers resort to flowery euphemisms or dress up the crude words as best they can.

But I am a writer.

The language barrier shall not defeat me.

I created my own "cheat sheet," a listing of descriptions for passion and desire. I filled a spiral notebook with verbs and some nouns for sexual intercourse, arousal, orgasm, male and female sexual organs, and other synonyms I'd need to keep from repeating myself. Over time, I added more and more words, until I released the first edition of *Naughty*

Naughty Words for Nice Writers

Words for Nice Writers in 2015. Because I'd gotten my start in publishing writing spanking romance, there was a large section in the thesaurus on spanking. Five years and two revisions later, *Naughty Words for Nice Writers* has been expanded to become a sex scene writing guide with even more categories, tips, and synonyms.

Naughty Words for Nice Writers, third edition, is not intended to provide an exhaustive list of sexual slang, but to offer *functional*, *usable* words for writers of romance, erotic romance, and erotica. Google the categories in this book and you'll find a plethora of slang, but the words will be ribald and unsuitable for romance writing. "Chicksicle," "Clamdigger," and "Gag mallet" as euphemisms for penis or "rusty axe wound" for vagina aren't romantic or erotic. So, I've curated the synonyms into lists writers can *use*. Whether a particular word is appropriate will depend on your subgenre, the tone, the point of view, and/or the characters.

How a group of men would refer to sex among themselves will differ from the way any one of them would speak to his girlfriend, and the language during the act would be different from dinner conversation. I've heard women refer to their vaginas as "vajayjay." I doubt a man has ever uttered the word. Because characters in erotic fiction often talk about sex besides engaging it, this thesaurus also contains words that would be used in conversation.

In writing this guide, I tried to create a natural flow. The beginning focuses on setting the mood and how to write a sex scene, the middle contains most of the word lists, and the latter part of the book is devoted to spanking. At the very end, please check out the "Naughty Words to Avoid," i.e. editing hacks I think you'll find useful.

If you think of words that should be in the thesaurus, please tell me! Email me at carabristol50(at)yahoo(dot)com.

Happy writing!

12 Tips for Writing Sex Scenes

I love what humorist and author Dave Barry wrote about sex. "As rule, women would like to devote as much time to foreplay and the sex act as men would like to devote to foreplay, the sex act, and building a garage." Here are some things to keep in mind when writing a sex scene.

1. Include a balance between action (the mechanical sex part, i.e. who does what to whom), description (of the characters, the setting, etc.), and dialogue.

2. Sex is more than mechanical motion. Bring sensation, thought, and emotion to the scene. Go beyond the physical to describe tactile details: does the act being performed feel warm, abrasive, smooth, tentative, or rough? What emotions does it conjure? What is your character thinking? Hint: it should be related to the plot. What changes for the characters

afterward? Does it cement their relationship or drive them farther apart?

3. A sex scene should contain three parts: seduction/foreplay, orgasm, and aftermath. Likewise, a spanking scene should have anticipation/dread, the discipline, and aftercare. Most of the word count should be devoted to the buildup. A sex scene should mirror the sex act itself: the "climax" is the shortest part. The longest part is the buildup to that point, which is followed by a resolution.

4. Make your sex scene about something other than sex. The physical intimacy is a metaphor for what is occurring in the relationship and should show character or advance the plot. He's leaving, and she's afraid she'll never see him again; he's a no-commitment kind of guy, but has come to realize he loves her. They're copulating like bunnies in heat because they're desperate, lonely, angry, frightened. He's not spanking her because she's been disobedient,

but because he fears for her safety if her misbehavior continues.

5. Decide on the tone of the encounter. Is it flirty, fun, frantic, rushed, sensual, raunchy, etc. Choose your words and metaphors from the tone. The tone of the sex scene should also fit the subgenre/tone of the book. A raunchy sex scene would be out of place in an otherwise sweet romance—unless of course, that's part of story, i.e. that you have goody-goody characters with a secret kinky lifestyle. The point is to have your sex scene fit with the overall tone and plot of the story.

6. Use dialog to move your scene. Strike a balance between the mundane utterances of "Oh God," and "Oh baby, oh baby" that people really utter and long, detailed conversations that would not occur in real life. Bring up some of those issues from No. 4.

7. Make good use of your *pre* and *post* coital conversations. Remember to advance the plot!

Have the characters speak about or internally reflect on the relationship.

8. Put a little kink in your scene or bring in a few props to add some spice and variety to the sex. Intercourse is pretty basic. If you start adding props, it gives you more to work with. Blindfold a character, have one character feed the other, tease the other with a feather, have them talk dirty to one another, etc.

9. Take it out of the bedroom. Sex on the sofa, in the shower, or on the dining table will add variety, but think beyond those still-common scenarios to something more unusual. I once had characters have sex in a tree. Again—the venue must fit the story.

10. In general, let your readers get to know your characters a bit before hopping into bed. Your readers will enjoy the sex scene more if they know and like the characters. A "rule of thumb" is that the first sex scene occurs about halfway through the book. Of course, that depends on the subgenre and the heat level of the romance.

The sex may occur much earlier in an erotic romance or much later in a tamer romance.

11. Avoid disembodied, independently moving body parts. Example. His hand drew loving circles over her clit. His hand caressed her face. The only hand I know of that can do that is Thing from *The Addams Family*. *He* drew loving circles over her clit. *He* caressed her face. Same rules apply to heads, eyes, mouths, lips, legs, etc. Exceptions exist, of course. One is if a movement is *truly* a reflexive action. So stomachs can clench, and heads can jerk. Another acceptable instance is when you want to convey the frantic or desperate nature of sex.

12. To keep your readers reading to the next chapter, don't end with the characters having "done it," end the chapter with the characters about to "do it."

Common Scents

Among the five senses, smell is often neglected. A fragrance can be a powerful attractant. (I once asked my cousin what attracted him to his wife when he met her, and he said the way she smelled. So there you have it.) Many "smells" can be used to describe taste (I don't recommend soap as one of those). The best choice of scents are those drawn from your character's situation. If she works at a bakery she might smell like cookies. If he's a lifeguard, he might smell like suntan lotion or the ocean. In describing scents you can be specific, e.g. roses or leather; more generic, e.g. fresh or clean; or emotional, e.g. comforting or enticing. With a few exceptions, the following list focuses on positive and neutral odors (Nobody wants a hero who smells like dirty gym socks or farts).

Antiseptic

Baby powder (For all those single dad/mom romances)

Bergamot (A men's citrus fragrance, often used in historical romance)

Chocolate

Cigarettes

Cigars

Naughty Words for Nice Writers

Cinnamon

Clean

Cloves

Coffee

Commanding

Coppery

Cum

Delicate

Delicious

Dog

Earthy

Faint

Feminine

Flowers

Fragrant

Fresh

Fresh cut grass

Heady

Heavy

Home

Hope

Horses

Lavender

Leather

Lemon

Lime

Manly

Masculine

Mint

Musky

Ocean

Oil or grease

Orange spice

Outdoorsy

Paint

Passion

Naughty Words for Nice Writers

Perspiration/sweat

Pine

Pool chlorine

Possibilities

Promise

Rain

Rich

Ripe

Roses

Savory

Seductive

Sex

Soap

Spicy

Strawberries

Sunshine

Suntan lotion

Sweet

Tangy

Tempting

Trouble

Vanilla

Warm

Wet dog (when that wolf shifter gets caught in the rain)

Wet earth

Whiskey

Womanly

Wood smoke

Woodsy

Synonyms for smell

Aroma

Balm

Bouquet

Naughty Words for Nice Writers

Cologne

Fragrance

Incense

Odor

Perfume

Redolence

Scent

Smoky

Stench

Stink

Trace

Voice Sounds

One of the first things the hero and heroine often notice about the other when they meet is how the other's voice sounds. (See also: Sexual noises)

Nouns for Voice

Accent

Baritone

Bark

Bass

Brogue

Chirp

Contralto

Drawl

Growl

Harmony

Intonation

Lungs (Often used in reference to singing or yelling, e.g., a strong set of lungs)

Melody

Monotone

Naughty Words for Nice Writers

Pitch

Purr

Sound

Speech

Tenor

Timbre

Tone

Twitter

Vibration

Vocalization

Vocals

Warble

Wheeze

Whisper

Adjectives for Voice

Be judicious in your use of adjectives. If you want to
say someone spoke in a whispery voice, why not say
she whispered?

Booming

Breathy

Brittle

Childlike

Croaky

Deep

Dulcet

Feminine

Flat

Fractured

Gentle

Girly

Gravelly

Gruff

Harsh

High

Hoarse

Honeyed

Husky

Lilting

Low

Manly

Masculine

Melodious

Musical

Naughty Words for Nice Writers

Nasal

Petulant

Powerful

Pure

Purring

Roaring

Rough

Silky

Shattered

Shrill

Singsong

Sleepy

Smooth

Somber

Sonorous

Strangled

Strong

Sweet

Thick

Thin

Throaty

Thunderous

Tremulous

Weak

Wheezy

Whiskey-soaked (Customize with your favorite alcoholic beverage)

Whispery/whispy

Wobbly

Descriptions for Appearance

Their eyes meet across a crowded room, and they think....what? Beauty is in the eye of the character. Although the hero and heroine *usually* think the other is attractive when they first meet, that's not always the case. In tropes like enemies to lovers or friends to lovers, assessments of physical attractiveness can change with their emotions. The hero might think the heroine is plain at first, but after he falls in love with her, he realizes how pretty she is. While you'll want to describe specific physical traits (eyes, hair, etc.) in more detail, here are some general adjectives for physical appearance.

Alien

Alluring

Alpha

Athletic

Average

Bald

Bearded

Beautiful

Becoming

Beefy

Beguiling

Bewitching

Blonde (f), Blond (m)

Bonny

Brawny

Broad

Buff

Built

Busty

Buxom

Captivating

Charming

Cheap

Comely

Curvy

Dark

Dazzling

Enchanting

Engaging

Naughty Words for Nice Writers

Fair

Feminine

Fine

Foxy

Full-figured

Furry

Glamorous

Glowering

Gorgeous

Graceful

Hairy

Handsome

Hardy

Hirsute

Homely

Hot

Hulking

Hunky

Husky

Imposing

Intriguing

Intoxicating

Irresistible

Leggy

Lithe

Lovely

Macho

Magnificent

Masculine

Mesmerizing

Model like

Muscular

Mysterious

Nondescript

Overdressed

Petite

Plain

Plump

Powerful

Pretty

Prime

Primo

Radiant

Raving (beauty)

Naughty Words for Nice Writers

Ravishing

Red-blooded

Rounded

Rugged

Scaled

Scary

Scarred

Seductive

Shapely

Short

Slender

Slim

Stocky

Stout

Strong

Stunning

Sexy

Sinewy

Strapping

Studly

Smokin'

Tall

Tanned

Tattooed

Tawdry

Toned

Tough

Trim

Ugly

Unassuming

Unattractive

Unkempt

Virile

Voluptuous

Well-groomed

Well-proportioned

Willowy

Winged

Winning

Wiry

Flirting 101

Your characters meet, they feel the chemistry, and they want to let the other person know they're interested. How do they do it?

Smiling

Asking for help

Playing dumb

Asking for a phone number

Offering their phone number

Slipping the person a note

Offering to teach the other person how to do something

Complimenting, especially about physical attributes

Entering the other person's personal space, moving closer

Looking upward through one's lashes (typically female)

Using a term of endearment or nickname

Wetting one's lips

Joking, making sexual innuendos

Touching, e.g. forearm, shoulder, "accidentally" brushing against the person

Showing off one's neck (a female behavior)

Laughing—typically the man demonstrates interest by trying to make the woman laugh, and the woman shows interest by laughing at his jokes. It's a time-honored tradition.

Giggling, acting silly

Making up excuses to see the person again

Making eye contact

Dressing seductively

Wearing something they know the other person likes

Showing an interest in the other person, asking questions

Doing favors for the other person

Sending flowers or other gifts

Using stupid pickup lines

Sexting

Feelings, Whoa, Oh, Oh, Feelings

They can run, but they can't hide from the feeling. Whether it's the warm-fuzzy emotion or red-hot sexual tension, here's what to call it:

Ache

Admiration

Adoration

Affection

Appetite

Ardor

Attraction

Besotted with

Bliss

Caring

Carnality

Closeness

Contentment

Craving

Crazy

Crushing on

Delight

Desire

Devotion

Dotes on

Ecstasy

Elation

Enjoyment

Esteem

Euphoria

Fervor

Fondness

Glee

Glow

Gratification

Hankering

Happiness

Have a soft spot for

Head over heels

Heat

Heaven

Hunger

Idolizes

Naughty Words for Nice Writers

In seventh heaven

Infatuation

Intensity

Intimacy

Joy

Joyfulness

Keenness

Languor

Longing

(The) L-word

Love

On cloud nine

Over the moon

Passion

Puppy love

Rapture

Regard

Respect

Rush

Satisfaction

Sensuousness

Sensuality

Sexuality

Strength

Sweetness

Tenderness

Thrill

Throb

Tingle

Want

Warmth

Yearning

Terms of Endearment

What are you going to call your hero/heroine? What do they call each other? What role do they play in the story? Remember, you can derive your own nicknames from your story, but here are terms of endearment and roles for your H/h.

Admirer, secret admirer

Angel

Arm candy

Babe

Bae

Baby

Babygirl

Ball and chain

Beau

Beautiful

Bed mate

Beloved

Betrothed

Better half

Blue eyes, brown eyes, bright eyes

Boo

Boy

Boyfriend

Bottom

Bride

Bridegroom

Broad

Bud

Buddy

Colleen

Chick

Companion

Concubine

Consort

Courtesan

Crush

Date

Darling

Dear

Dude

Doll

Naughty Words for Nice Writers

Dom (male)

Dominant

Domme (female)

Eye candy

Flame

Fiancé (male)

Fiancée (female)

Friend

Friend with benefits

Gal

Gentleman, gentleman caller

Gold digger

Gigolo

Girl

Girlfriend

Groom

(My) heart

Heartbreaker

Heartthrob

Hoh, head of household

Hon, hun

Honey

Hubby

Husband

Ingénue

Intended

Jailbait

Keeper

King

Lady, lady friend

Lass

Lover

Love

Lover boy

Maiden

Main squeeze

(My) man

Master

Miss

Mister

Mistress

Number, e.g., she's a hot little number

(The) one

Old maid

Naughty Words for Nice Writers

Old man

Old lady

One and only

One that got away

Paramour

Partner

Pet

Prince

Prince Charming

Princess

Pumpkin

Queen

Sex partner

Skirt

Soulmate

Spouse

Steady

Sugar

Suitor

Sweetheart

Sweetie

Sweetie pie

Virgin

Wife

Wifey

Sheila

Sub

Subbie

Submissive

Top

Wench

(My) woman

Lust

This is how it all begins, isn't it? Let's call sexual desire what it is…

Ache

Anticipation

Appetite

Ardor

Arousal

Biological urge

Carnality

Concupiscence

Craving

Craze

Cupidity

Debauchery

Desire

Dissolution

Drive

Eagerness

Excitement

Fervor

Fire

Getting frisky

Getting hard

Getting wet

Heat

Horniness

Hots

Hunger

Inferno

Intemperance

Interest

Intoxication

Lasciviousness

Lechery

Lewdness

Libido

Need

Pang

Passion

Pleasure

Profligacy

Naughty Words for Nice Writers

Promiscuity

Prurience

(In) Rut

Sex drive

Sensuousness

Take a liking to

Tension

Thirst

Thrill

Want

Wantonness

Urge

Urgency

Yearning

Kiss

Ah, the kiss. That perfect expression of love, lust, and romance for which there are surprisingly few synonyms. So we resort to euphemistic oral calisthenics.

Nouns for Kiss

Buss

Caress

Contact

French kiss

Osculate (only Sheldon of *The Big Bang Theory* would be likely to use this one)

Liplock

Making out (includes petting)

Necking (involves petting also)

Peck

Smooch

Touch

Verbs for Kiss

Most of these words need nouns (mouths, lips) to convey the act of kissing. But beware disembodied, independently moving parts. Lips and mouths should not be allowed to wander off on their own. Example: *His mouth fused to hers.* Really? Without any action or thought on his part, his mouth attached itself to her? That's pretty scary. Better: He fused his mouth to hers. Of course, depending on context, there may be exceptions.

Bite

Brush

Burn

Capture

Caress

Claim

Coax

Connect

Cover

Crush

Dance

Devour

Duel

Glance

Glide

Graze

Greet

Grind

Entice

Explore

Fasten

Fuse

Knit

Knot

Lay a liplock on

Lick

Lave

Lock on

Loom

Mash

Mate

Meet

Naughty Words for Nice Writers

Nibble

Nip

Nuzzle

Peck

Plant

Play

Plunder

Press

Ravage

Rub

Sample

Savor

Seduce

Settle

Slant

Slide

Smash

Smooch

Spar

Suck

Tangle

Tango

Taste

Tease

Tempt

Touch

Toy

Location, Location, Location

The bedroom is the obvious and most common place to make love, but *where* your characters have sex affects *how* they have sex. Certain positions will be easier or more difficult (or impossible) to assume. A private act may turn exhibitionist. Available props can facilitate or hinder activity. If you want to spice things up, consider moving your lovers out of the bedroom.

Kitchen – counter, table, floor, pantry

Living room – sofa, floor, armchair, in front of the fireplace, on an animal skin rug, on a grand piano (suggest lowering the lid first)

Bathroom – shower, bathtub, floor

In someone else's bedroom

Front porch, patio

Roof

Swimming pool, hot tub

Office – boardroom, boss's office, elevator

Library

Health spa/gym/locker room

Store dressing room

Model home

In a treehouse, tree

In a tent

In a sleeping bag

In the car on a private lane, in the vehicle on a public street

At the police station

In the hospital

While on the telephone

In a restaurant

In a bar

Parking lot

At someone else's house

On the beach

At a drive-in movie (hey, it could be a *historical* romance)

At a "walk-in" movie theater

In the garage

At a BDSM club

On an airplane

On a bus, train, boat

Naughty Words for Nice Writers

On a gondola

At a hotel

Against the window

At home with drapes open, lights on

In an abandoned warehouse

On a spaceship

On a space station

In a cave

At the character's workplace

In a cemetery

On a tour bus

In a horse-drawn carriage

In a barn

At a park

In a gazebo

In a senator's office

In the Oval office

In prison

Bedroom Basics – Setting the Scene

So, your characters didn't want to have sex in the neighbor's treehouse while guests enjoyed the barbecue on the patio, but played it safe by doing the deed in their very own bedroom. What you tell about the bedroom can enhance or diffuse the eroticism. How much detail you use in describing the room depends on your plot and the mood you wish to convey. Some details matter; some don't. If the sheets are plain cotton, it may not matter. If they're satin, and the couple slide all over the place and the hero hits his head on the wall, then fabric content matters. If the heroine finds another woman's undies in the bed, that's a detail worth mentioning. Here are some factors to consider in setting the scene:

- Is the bedroom messy or neat? Overly decorated or minimalist?
- Is the bed made? Are there dozens of pillows to toss aside or do they just rip back the coverlet?

- Do they bother to pull back the bedspread or just fall on the bed and go at it?

- What kind of sheets are on the bed?

- Are the drapes open or closed?

- Is the window open or closed? Can someone hear them? Do they hear the neighbor's lawn mower while they're having sex?

- Lights on or off?

- Music on or music off?

- TV on or TV off?

- Are they watching porn?

- What kind of bed? Canopied? Waterbed? King or Twin?

- What does the bed feel like? Is it firm? Soft? Are the covers/sheets silky or scratchy?

- Room temperature. Is it hot so that they fling off the covers? Or cold so that they huddle beneath them?

- Do they make it to the bed or have sex on the floor?

- What does the room smell like? Scented candles? Dirty socks? His cologne? His former girlfriend's perfume? The roses from outside the open window?

- What's on the nightstand? Pick items that show something about the character who lives there).

- What's on the floor? (Again, use this detail to show character or advance the plot).

- Where do they have to go for a condom? The nightstand drawer? Is there a box on the bedside table? Is it in the hero's wallet? Do they have to grab one from the bathroom?

- Who else is in the house? Do they have to be quiet?

- Are the walls so thin they fear the neighbors will hear?

- Is there a phone in the room? Do they shut it off or risk letting it ring?

- What's on the ceiling?

- Is there something in the room unique to the character? Does the heroine have her extensive doll collection on display? Does the nerdy guy hero have superhero bedsheets? Is grandma

staring at them from the picture over the bed?
Are there sex toys lying around?

To reiterate: Don't go overboard on the details to the extent that it slows the action. Many details don't matter. Use only the ones that do.

Getting Naked

The clothing has to come off (well, some of it, anyway). So how are they going to remove it? Will it be sensual or frantic? Do they remove their own clothing or undress their partner? Lots of decisions to make, and lots of ways to say get naked.

How to Remove Clothing

Drop (e.g. trousers)

Expose (a body part)

Fling

Kick off

Let a garment puddle or pool

Loosen (a robe, a belt)

Open (a robe)

Peel off

Pull

Release (such as a towel, a robe around the shoulders, etc.)

Rip off

Shed

Naughty Words for Nice Writers

Shimmy out of

Shrug off

Slip off, out of

Tear off

Toe off (socks or shoes)

Toss

Tug off

Wiggle out of

Wrestle out of

Undo

Unbutton

Unfasten

Unsnap

Untie

Unzip

Generic Verbs for Getting Naked

When how isn't as important as getting there…

Bare

Get out of one's clothing

Get naked

Disrobe

Divest

Doff

Drop trow, drawers, clothing

Remove clothing

Reveal

Shed

Strip

Undress

Uncover

Synonyms for Naked

Au naturel

Bare

Buck naked

Birthday suit

Exposed

In dishabille

In the altogether

In the buff

In the raw

Indecent

Nakedness

Naughty Words for Nice Writers

Nude

Stripped

Unclad

Unclothed

Undressed

Wearing only a smile

Without a stitch on

Four Phases of Sexual Response

Physiologically there are four phases to human sexual response: excitement, plateau, orgasm, and resolution (Source: WebMd). In fiction, these phases often are condensed to three: excitement, orgasm, and resolution—and some authors end a scene with orgasm, thus reducing it to two phases. But it is helpful to know what occurs physiologically so you can accurately describe it (in erotic language, of course).

Excitement

- Muscles tense.
- Heart rate and respiration increase.
- Chest and back may flush/turn blotchy (sex flush).
- Nipples harden and become erect.
- Blood flow to the genitals increases, resulting in the inner and outer labia becoming swollen in women, and in erection in men.
- Vaginal lubrication begins.

- Breasts and vaginal walls swell.
- Testicles swell, the scrotum tightens, and pre-ejaculate fluid is secreted (precum).

Plateau

- Vagina continues to swell. The clitoris becomes highly sensitive and retracts under the clitoral hood.
- Testicles retract into the scrotum.
- Heart rate and breathing continue to increase.
- Muscle tension increases even more with possible spasms in the feet, hands, and face

Orgasm

- Heart rate and breathing are at their highest.
- Vaginal muscles and uterus contract.
- Muscles in the feet spasm (toes curl!).
- Muscles contract at the base of the penis causing ejaculation.
- The "sex flush" may appear over the entire body.

Resolution

- The body returns to its normal state.

- Feelings of well-being, intimacy, and/or sleepiness may ensue.

- With additional stimulation, some women can achieve another orgasm ("multiple orgasms"), however, men enter a "refractory" or recovery period before they're good to go again. The refractory period increases with age. (In young men, this stage can be only minutes. In older men, it can be days).

Sexual Positions

Sexual positions are like fiction genres. There are a limited number of basic ones, but when you "mix and match" or add a few variations, you create numerous subgenres.

Missionary

Woman on top, face-to-face

Side-by-side, face-to-face

Side-by-side, front to back ("spooning")

Doggy style

Sitting

Standing

Reverse cowgirl, woman straddling reclining partner, facing away from him

Sixty-nine (oral sex)

Sexual Acts

Possibilities abound to jazz up a sex scene. Some of these acts lean toward erotica rather than romance. Many forms of kink are labeled "play."

Age play

Anal sex

Analingus (rimming)

Bondage

Breath play

Cunnilingus

Discipline

Domination

Dressing provocatively, or in costume

Exhibitionism

Fantasizing

Fellatio

Flashing

Flirting

Fisting

Naughty Words for Nice Writers

Fondling/Petting

Ginger figging

Hand job

Intercourse

Kissing

Masturbation

Ménage

Orgasm restriction/edging

Phone Sex

Pony Play

Recording yourselves having sex

Role Play

(Use of) Sex toys

Sexting

Spanking

Swinging (Wife swapping)

Taking naked pictures

Talking dirty

Twerking

Voyeurism

Watching porn

Wax play

Foreplay

How do I touch thee? Let me count the ways.

Anoint

Bathe

Bite

Bump

Capture

Caress

Circle

Claim

Clasp

Claw

Cling

Coddle

Collide

Connect (with)

Cuddle

Cup

Dance

Naughty Words for Nice Writers

Delve

Embrace

Entice

Examine

Explore

Feather

Finger

Flick

Flirt

Flutter

Fondle

Go down on

Grasp

Graze

Grope

Heat

Hold

Hug

Inspect

Jack off

Kiss

Knead

Lave

Lash

Lick

Love

Massage

Masturbate

Mingle

Nestle

Nip

Nudge

Nuzzle

Meet

Paint

Palm

Pat

Pet

Pinch

Play

Pluck

Press

Propel

Pull

Naughty Words for Nice Writers

Pull back

Pull near

Pump

Punish

Push

Rasp

Relish

Retract

Roll

Rub

Savor

Scrap

Scratch

Seize

Skate

Skim

Skip (over)

Skitter

Slap

Slide

Squeeze

Sting

Stroke

Study

Sweep

Tap

Taste

Tease

Tempt

Tongue

Torment

Torture

Toy

Tremble (e.g., her hand trembled on…)

Tweak

Twist

Vanquish

Warm

Oral Sex

As foreplay or in lieu of sexual intercourse, for him and for her, here are some words to know.

Blow

Bump the back of the throat

Consume

Cover (one's sex)

Deep throat

Draw (into one's mouth)

Eat

Engulf (into one's mouth)

Fellate

Flick

Flicker

Fuck face

Give head

Go down on

Hollow one's cheeks

Kiss

Lash

Lave

Lick

Rub

Savor

Sit on one's face

Sixty-nine

Suck

Suck off

Swirl

Taste

Take in one's mouth

Tongue

Intercourse

The in-and-out mechanics. These words can apply to either coitus or anal sex. Some refer to the initial entry, while others to the motion.

Bang

Batter

Become/get intimate

Boink

Breech

Buck

Bump and grind

Bury

Caress

Claim

Consummate

Copulate

Couple

Delve

Diddle

Do it

Do the nasty

Drill

Drive

Ease (into, onto)

Engage/have marital relations

Enter

Fool around

Fornicate

Fuck

Get laid

Get nasty

Go all the way

Guide (one's penis)

Gyrate

Hammer

Hump

Impale

Insert

Invade

Join

Lay

Naughty Words for Nice Writers

Lower (oneself onto)

Lunge

Make love

Make whoopee

Mate

Merge

Move

Nail

Nudge

Penetrate

Piston

Plunge

Poke

Pound

Press (into)

Probe

Prod

Push

Race

Ram

Ravish

Ride

Rock

Rush

Score

Screw

Seat (oneself)

Shag

Shove

Sink (into, onto)

Sleep with

Slide

Sodomize (anal sex)

Stroke

Surge

Swivel (hips)

Take

Thrust

Orgasm

If your POV character is coming, you can describe the sensation, the physical response, and the dialog uttered (Oh God, Oh God…). If your POV character is noting his or her *partner's* state you can remark on the visuals.

Nouns for Orgasm

Agony

Apex of Desire

Big O

Bliss

Climax

Coming

Completion

Crescendo

Ecstasy

End

Explosion

Fire

Gratification

Happy ending

High

Hurricane

Inferno

Joy

Little death

Nirvana

Oblivion

Paroxysm of pleasure

Peak

Pinnacle

Pleasure

Point of no return (Sensation of orgasm being

imminent)

Rapture

Release

Rush

Satisfaction

Sensation

Storm

Naughty Words for Nice Writers

Tornado

Vortex

Whirlwind

Verbs for Orgasm

Some of these words pair with nouns (A climax ripped through her) or can be used alone (She climaxed). Others describe physiological responses to show rather than tell one is experiencing an orgasm.

Blaze (all the fire words)

Blow one's load

Burgeon

Carry away

Climax

Coil

Come (Often in erotic romance *come* is the verb; *cum* is the noun for the secretion. This varies by publisher.)

Contort

Contract (muscles, walls, channels, etc.)

Convulse

Ejaculate

Empty onesself

Erupt

Naughty Words for Nice Writers

Expend

Explode

Fall

Finish

Fire off

Fly

Get off

Hurtle

Pound

Pump

Rip

Roar

Rocket

Rush

Shatter

Shoot

Skyrocket

Snap

Soar

Spew (cum)

Spill

Spin (spin out of control, head spins, etc.)

Squirt (most often used to describe female orgasm resulting from G-spot manipulation)

Storm

Surrender

Swell

Sweep

Tear

Tense

Tumble

Uncoil

Whip

Whirl

Cum (noun, the ejaculate)

Bodily Fluid

Cream

Fluid

Ejaculate

Elixir (generally fantasy romances)

Emission

Essence

Naughty Words for Nice Writers

Honey (used for females only)

Jism

Jizz

Moisture

Nectar

Precum (the fluid secreted by males before orgasm.

Alternative spelling: pre-cum.)

Seed

Semen

Seminal fluid

Spunk

Wad

Wetness

What People Do When They're Coming

Arch their necks

Arch their backs

Bang head on the headboard

Beg

Bellow

Bite their partners (common in vampire and wolf shifter stories)

Clench/contract facial muscles

Collapse (e.g., legs give out)

Contract (such as pussies, wombs, testicles, and cocks)

Convulse

Curl their toes (this really happens)

Curse, swear

Dig their hands into their partners' hips, shoulders

Ejaculate

Flush, blush, turn red

Gasp

Grit their teeth

Grab bedclothes in their fists

Naughty Words for Nice Writers

Grab bedpost

Groan

Growl

Howl

Lose control

Make faces

Moan

Open their eyes

Open their mouths (e.g., form an "O")

Perspire

Pulse (clits, pussies, and cocks)

Say "Oh God"

Say their partner's name

Say the wrong name

See stars (common in erotic romance)

See fireworks (common in romance)

Shout

Shudder

Shut their eyes

Tense, stiffen

Twitch

Throw their heads back

Thrust one final time

Wake the neighbors

Writhe

Sexual Aftermath

Many authors end a sex scene with orgasm; however, if you read the section on the four stages of sexual response, you know orgasm is not the end of the sexual cycle. There is the cooling down period when everything returns to normal—or perhaps not, depending on your story. What your characters say and do during this period should advance your plot or give more insight into who they are as people or what they want out of the relationship. So what do people do after sex?

Apologize

Agonize over the relationship

Analyze the relationship

Bask in the glow

Break up

Check on the kids

Check their phone, email

Clean up, take a shower

Come to their senses

Confess their love

Confess something other than love

Cuddle, spoon

Daydream/think

Dispose of the condom

Eat/have dinner

Fall asleep

Gasp for breath

Get dressed

Go for round two!

Go to work

Hang up the phone (phone sex)

Hide/put away the sex toys

Fall asleep

Laugh together

Let the dog in

Lie in silence

Make a fast exit

Profess their love

Put on their jammies

Rate the experience (Either silently, or they ask their partner)

Naughty Words for Nice Writers

Regret what he/she just did

Share secrets

Shut off the TV

Smoke a cigarette

Snuggle

Suffer regrets, doubt, guilt, jealousy

Talk, have a heart-to-heart (in romance, this discussion should further the plot).

Turn on the TV

Turn off the video camera

Uncuff/untie their partner

Wonder what the other person is thinking

Worry about pregnancy

Sexual Noises

Keep in mind the sex and personality traits of the character uttering the sound. Some noises are gender neutral; others are not. A woman might squeak or squeal. A macho hero will not. Likewise, the soft and feminine heroine is not likely to bellow during sex. Included in this list are some room sounds. (See also voice sounds).

Bang

Bark

Bellow

Blubber

Choke

Cry, weep

Crash

Creak

Gasp

Giggle

Groan

Naughty Words for Nice Writers

Growl

Grumble

Grunt

Hiss

Howl

Hum

Keen

Moan

Murmur

Mutter

Pant

Roar

Rumble

Scream

Shout

Shriek

Sigh

Slurp

Snarl

Squeak

Squeal

Squish

Thud

Thump

Thunder

Wail

Wheeze

Whimper

Whine

Whisper

Yell

Yelp

Penis

With the quantity and descriptive value of synonyms for this noble organ, you would think people do nothing but sit around and talk about dicks all day. Note that some terms are general (groin), some are specific (erection), and others refer to specific parts of the penis (shaft, corona). Keep in mind that some men have pet names for their penises, so, within the right context, you can make up your own names.

Bulge

Big Jim (substitute character's name)

Breadth

Cap

Circumference

Cock

Cockhead

Corona

Crown

Crotch

Dick

Erection

Flesh

Foreskin

Genitals

Girth

Groin

Hard-on

Head

Heat-seeking missile

"Him" (she stroked him)

Johnson

Joystick

Length

Little Jim (substitute character's name)

Loins

Manflesh

Manhood

Manroot

Member

One-eyed lizard

Organ

Naughty Words for Nice Writers

Package (generally refers to penis and testicles as a unit)

Pecker

Peter

Phallus

Prick

Privates

Ridge

Rod

Shaft

Skin

Soldier

Spittin' lizard

Staff

Stalk

Stiffy

Tallywacker

Thickness

Third leg

Tool

Tumescence

Underside

Wood

Woody

Adjectives to describe an erection

Let us admire thee!

Aroused

Bulging

Curved

Engorged

Erect

Excited

Full

Hard

Impressive

Long

Massive

Proud

Pulsating

Pulsing

Rock hard

Smooth

Steely

Naughty Words for Nice Writers

Stiff

Stony, stone hard

Thick

Throbbing (tends to be clichéd)

Tumescent

Veiny

Testicles

Some of these entries refer to the testicles, others to the scrotum that contains them.

Balls

Ball sac

(The) boys

Cajones

Family jewels

Gonads

Groin (the general area)

Huevos

Nads

Nuts

Sac

Scrotum

Stones

Testes

Vagina

Words for vagina tend to be less defined than synonyms for penis. Vagina words frequently refer to the general location rather than the sex organ itself. Compare dick, peter, cock with apex of her thighs, lady bits, core. It is as if we've developed an entire vocabulary to avoid referring to the vagina.

Apex of her thighs

Area

Between her legs, thighs

Canal

Center

Channel

Cleft

Core

Crease

Crotch

Cunt

Cunny

Delta of Venus

Down south

(The) Duchess

Entrance

Folds

Flesh

Furrow

Gash

Genitalia

Genitals

Girl parts

G-spot

Heat

"Her"

Hole

Honey

Honey pot

Hoohah

Inside

Labia

Lady bits

Lady business

Naughty Words for Nice Writers

Lady Jane

Lady parts

Mark

Miss Priss

Mons

Muff

Nether lips

Nether yaya

Petals

Portal

Pudendum

Privates

Pussy

Quim

Region

Sheath

Slickness

Slit

Snatch

Target

Tightness

Tissue

Treasure

Twat

Vag

Vajayjay

Vee (between her legs)

Velvet curtain

Vulva

Warmth

Wet heat

Wetness

Womanhood

The P word v. the C word

Pussy or cunt? Which is better? Which is more acceptable? Answer: It's totally up to you. Readers and authors are divided. Some people hate the C word and prefer the P word. Others prefer the C word and dislike the P word. Pick your preference—or use a different word. I gave you a list of synonyms!

Naughty Words for Nice Writers

Do not ever describe a vagina as moist. Moist is universally disliked, which is why it's not on the following list. People also dislike creaming.

Descriptions for arousal

Note: See also the Four Stages of Sexual Response

Achy

Awakened

Aroused

Clenching

Contracting

Damp

Dewy

Drenched

Engorged

Excited

Feeling of heaviness, fullness

Fluttering

Hot

Letting down moisture (ok to use in this context)

Panties get wet, drenched, damp, etc.

Pulsing

Responded

Slick

Sopping

Swollen

Tightens

Throbbing

Weeping

Wet

Clitoris

The clitoris is often described with a noun plus adjective or a phrase: Center of sensation, bundle of nerves, etc.

Bud

Bundle of nerves

Button

Center

Clit

Clitty

Clitoral hood

Core

Flesh

Gem

Hood

Jewel

Love button

Nerve center

Nodule

Nub

Nubbin

Pearl

Pleasure center

Sensation center

Tissue

Breasts

Balloons

Bee stings

Boobies

Boobs

Bosom

Bumps

Bust

Chest

Cleavage

Curves

Flesh

(The) Girls

Globes

Headlights

Hemispheres

Hood ornaments

Hooters

Jugs

Knockers

Mammaries

Melons, honeydews, peaches, apples, pears (pick your fruit)

Mounds

Orbs

Pair

Peaks (often used for nipples)

Pillows

Puppies

Rack

Rounds

Set

Speed bumps

Tatas

Tits

Titties

Torpedoes

(The) Twins

Weight

Winnebagos

Nipples

Aureole (not the actual nipple)

Beads

Berries

Buds

Bullets

High Beams

Nips

Peaks

Pebbles

Raspberries

Teats

Tips

Buttocks

Area

Arse (British)

Ass

Back end

Backside

Badonkadonk

Behind

Bootie

Bottom

Bum (British)

Buns

Butt

Buttocks

Caboose

Cheeks

Crease

Culo (Italian)

Derriere

End zone

Naughty Words for Nice Writers

Fanny

Flesh

Globes

Glutes (shortened version for the gluteus maximus muscles)

Hiney

Keister

Moons

Posterior

Rear

Rump

Seat

Sit-spot (the crease, where thigh meets butt)

Skin

Surface

Hide

Tail

Target

Tuchus (Yiddish)

Tush

Tushy (tushie)

Anus

In writing about anal sex or anal play, anus and rectum often are used interchangeably, and it gets the message across. But, technically, the anus is the opening while rectum is the canal. This part of the anatomy is often described by using a noun denoting an opening preceded by a specific modifier: *back entrance*, *puckered entrance*. You can achieve variety by mixing and matching nouns and adjectives—but don't overdo it.

Anal opening
Anus
Arse (British)
Arsehole (British)
Ass
Asshole
Back hole
Back door

Naughty Words for Nice Writers

Bum (technically buttocks, but, in context, it can be used for anus)

Bottom hole

Brown hole

Bunghole

Butt hole

Passage, Back passage

Canal

Channel

Nether region

Opening

Orifice

Portal

Private hole

Puckered entrance

Rectum

Rosebud

Rosette

Sphincter

Tightness

Untamed hole

Virgin hole

All Those Other Body Parts

You can say *nose*, *eats*, *mouth*, or *hand* and no one blinks an eye. But call attention to someone's penis or vagina, and you've committed a social faux pas. Interestingly enough, there are few words for socially acceptable body parts, but many euphemisms and slang terms for the private ones. We have developed a secret vocabulary to talk about what we're not supposed to mention. But since sex involves more than sex organs, I offer a short list from other parts:

Arm – limb, appendage, biceps (always plural), upper arm, elbow, crook (of the arm), lower arm, forearm, wrist

Back – spine, slope, shoulders

Chest – torso, pecs, wall, front, trunk

Ear – shell, auricle, ear lobe, lobe

Eye – orb (rarely), eyeballs, baby blues, peepers, eyebrow, brow, eyelash, lash, eyelid, lid, pupil, iris, whites, schlera

Mouth – lips, seam (of the lips) kisser, recess, cavity, yap, trap, chops, tongue, teeth, palate, throat

Muscles – Hardbody, musculature, physique, sinews, brawn, beefiness, stockiness, biceps, guns, abs, six pack, washboard, pecs, glutes, quads. *Adjectives*: hard, chiseled, sculpted, iron, steely, rugged, ripped, rippled, wiry, beefy, firm, stout, taut, toned, bulging, ropy, powerful, hulking, strong, burly

Face – features, appearance, mask, countenance, mug, profile, visage, expression, cheeks, apples (of the cheeks), chin, jaw, jawline

Foot – extremity, hoof, sole, instep, arch, toes, tootsies

Hair – tresses, locks, strands, hairdo, "do," coiffure, style, curls, mane, frizz, fringe, bangs, fuzz, mop, haircut, fur, braid, ponytail, bun, updo, shock, thatch, tuft, comb-over, cowlick, cornrow, afro, sideburns, dreadlocks, bob, chignon, perm, mohawk, length, corkscrews, spirals, ringlets, pigtails, bouffant, crewcut, buzz cut, flip, fibers, wool, silk

For facial hair – beard, whiskers, scruff, five o'clock shadow, shadow, stubble, peach fuzz, bristles, goatee, soul patch, mustache

Hand – fist, palm, back of the hand, extremity, paw, mitt, ham, hooker, shaker, right one, left one, fingers, digits, forefinger, index finger, pointer finger, ring finger, middle finger, thumb, pinkie, knuckles, wrist

Head – forehead, temple, skull, crown, dome, pate, scalp, noggin

Leg – limb, gam, appendage, thigh, quads, knee, kneecap, calf, shin, ankle

Neck – throat, scruff, collar, nape, curve, slope

Nose – sometimes you can get away with using beak. But a nose is a nose. Nostrils.

Stomach – abdomen, abs, six-pack, tummy, belly, gut, midriff, midsection, middle, paunch, spare tire, washboard, navel, belly button

Sexual Metaphors

To write a sex scene that is unique to your story, draw your inspiration from what your characters do out of bed or what is important to them and base your sexual word usage on that. For example, if your character likes to swim, you could use words like diving, breaststroke, skinny dipping, etc. Make sure the metaphor applies to your story, and don't overdo it or you'll end up with a parody. Sprinkle in the metaphors. Here are some general ones to get you thinking:

Animal themes (clawing, purring, roaring, scratching)
Battling/Fighting (pounding, pummeling, claiming)
Business (mergers and acquisitions, hostile takeover,)
Dancing (tango, gliding, waltzing, dirty dancing)
Domination (subjugating, spanking, claiming)
Fire (heat, blaze, smoldering embers, conflagration)
Fireworks (skyrockets, seeing stars, lighting a fuse)
Intoxication (feeling drunk, staggering, reeling)

Music (crescendo, cymbals crashing, a drumming heartbeat)

Mythological/magical (siren song, love potions, being enchanted, being bewitched)

Nature (having butterflies, blooming, flowering, dew, nectar)

Occupational themes (a doctor's bedside manner, playing doctor; an artist who paints the body, uses gentle or bold strokes, etc.)

Outer space (supernovas, thrusters, exploding stars, planetary rotation)

Sports (scoring, slam dunk, end run, getting to first base, hitting a homerun)

Storms (tornados, hurricanes, heatwave, vortexes)

Water (waves crashing, a flood, plunging, in over one's head)

A to Z Active Sex Verbs

The key to using this list effectively is to be creative. One can bask in desire, be bombarded by it, have it coil in the pit of one's stomach, swell with it, succumb to it…you get the picture.

Abandon

Abrade

Accommodate

Ache

Ambush

Amplify

Anoint

Arouse

Assault

Attract

Awaken

Bask

Beat

Bite

Blast

Bloom

Blossom

Bombard

Bump

Burn

Captivate

Capture

Careen

Caress

Cascade

Cast a spell

Chafe

Charge

Charm

Chase

Circle

Cling

Coax

Coil

Collide

Command

Naughty Words for Nice Writers

Consume

Control

Course

Covet

Cradle

Crash

Crave

Crawl

Cream

Crush

Curl

Cut

Dampen

Dance

Dash

Delight

Deliver

Delve

Demand

Destroy

Detonate

Devastate

Dew

Dissolve

Dominate

Douse

Drag

Drape

Draw

Drench

Drip

Drown (in)

Drug

Duel

Echo

Electrify

Elicit

Embrace

Energize

Enliven

Ensnare

Entice

Entrance (meaning charm, not an entry)

Entwine

Naughty Words for Nice Writers

Envelope

Escalate

Exhale

Explode

Explore

Falter

Fan

Feast

Feed

Fire up

Flash

Flaunt

Flee

Flip

Flirt

Flit

Flood

Floor

Flower

Flush

Flutter

Fly

Fondle

Force

Gallop

Glory (in)

Gnaw

Grab

Grapple

Grasp

Grind

Grope

Grovel

Grow

Guide

Gyrate

Hammer

Harden

Haul

Heat

Heave

Heighten

Hesitate

Hex

Naughty Words for Nice Writers

Hold

Home in on

Hug

Hum

Humble

Humiliate

Hunger

Hurtle

Ignite

Impale

Implode

Inch

Incinerate

Indulge

Inflame (also enflame)

Inhale

Inspire

Intoxicate

Itch

Jab

Jerk

Join

Jolt

Jump

Kindle

Kiss

Knead

Kneel

Knife

Lash

Lay waste

Lean against, on

Let down (moisture)

Light

Love

Lure

Manhandle

Manipulate

March

Marshal

Massage

Maul

Meander

Melt

Naughty Words for Nice Writers

Mimic

Moisten

Mold

Molest

Mount

Muster

Nail

Nip

Nurture

Nudge

Nuzzle

Open

Overload

Overrule

Overrun

Overwhelm

Panic

Pause

Parry

Penetrate

Perspire

Pierce

Play

Plunge

Polish

Pool

Pounce

Pound

Pour

Pray

Puddle

Pull

Pulsate

Pulse

Pummel

Pump

Quake

Quell

Quench

Quicken

Quiver

Race

Rage

Rain

Naughty Words for Nice Writers

Rake

Ram

Rally

Rasp

Ratchet

Ravish

React

Reconnoiter

Recoup

Recover

Reel

Refuse

Regain

Reject

Rejoice

Relinquish

Repeat

Respond

Retaliate

Resist

Resound

Ricochet

Rip

Risk

Run (wild, rampant, amok etc.)

Salute

Sap

Sate

Satisfy

Saturate

Savage

Scald

Scoot

Scorch

Scrape

Scrub

Sear

Seduce

Seize

Send

Shake

Shiver

Short-circuit

Shred

Naughty Words for Nice Writers

Shudder

Shun

Sigh

Simmer

Sizzle

Singe

Sink

Skip

Skim

Skitter

Skyrocket

Slacken

Slake

Slap

Sluice

Smash

Smell

Sniff

Snuggle

Soar

Somersault

Spank

Spark

Spasm

Spike

Spin

Spread

Spring

Startle

Stir

Strike

Strut

Stumble

Stun

Subdue

Submerge

Succumb

Suck

Surrender

Swagger

Swallow

Sway

Swell

Swipe

Naughty Words for Nice Writers

Swirl

Tackle

Tangle

Tear

Tempt

Thirst

Thrill

Throb

Thumb

Thunder

Thrust

Thrum

Tingle

Torment

Torture

Touch

Trace

Trail

Transmit

Transport

Treasure

Trickle

Twist

Undulate

Unfetter

Unfold

Unleash

Untangle

Vanquish

Vault

Vibrate

Violate

Wage an assault

Wander

Ward (off)

Wash

Wave

Weaken

Weave

Wedge

Whack

Whip

Whirl

Wiggle

Naughty Words for Nice Writers

Worship

Wreak havoc

Wrench

Yearn

Yield

Zap

Zero in on

Zing

Zip

Spanking Section

Spanking could have its own thesaurus! In this section, you'll find synonyms for all things spanking. Reasons to spank:

Discipline

Eroticism (play)

Maintenance

Reinforce dominant and submissive roles

Relieve stress

Spanking Verbs

Keep in the mind the tone and reason for your scene. A spanking can be playful or punishing. Light or severe. Intensity should grow. If you *start out* by blistering, you'll box yourself in. Weave in description, dialog, thoughts, and emotions with the action.

Assault

Blister

Bounce

Brand

Burn

Cane

Caress

Chasten

Chastise

Compress

Connect (hand to ass)

Crack

Crush (one's cheeks)

Deliver

Discipline

Flatten

Flog

Glance (a blow)

Graze

Heat

Hit

Inflict

Kiss

Lash

Lay (into)

Light a fire

Light into

Make glow

Make rosy

Make blush

Meet (as in hand meets ass)

Nail

Paddle

Paint

Pinken

Naughty Words for Nice Writers

Punish

Redden

Roast

Sear

Scorch

Slap

Smack

Snap

Spank

Sting

Streak

Strike

Stripe

Suffuse (with color)

Swat

Tan

Tease

Tenderize

Thrash

Thwack

Tint

Toast

Transmit (pain)

Turn rosy

Wallop

Warm

Welt

Whack

Whale (into)

Whip

Whup

Descriptions for Ass

How many ways can you describe the appearance of an ass before, during, and after a spanking? A lot, if you move beyond color. Keep in mind the POV! Spankees (bottoms) can feel pain, but until they look, they won't know their asses are red—that is something only the spanker (top) can see.

Aching

Ample

Apple (cheeks)

Beautiful

Blooming

Blushing

Bountiful

Branded

Bright

Broad

Bruised

Burning

Cherry (red)

Colored

Creamy

Crimson

Curvy

Dimpled

Fiery

Firm

Flat

Flattened

Florid

Flush

Flushed

Glorious

Glowing

High

Inflamed

Jiggling

Low

Marked

Muscled

Naughty

Naughty Words for Nice Writers

Pale

Peach, peachy

Pert

Pink

Pillowy

Proud

Red, reddened

Rose, rosy

Round

Ruby

Ruddy

Sagging

Sassy

Saucy

Scarlet

Sensitive

Sexy

Shelf-like

Skinny

Smarting

Soft

Splotchy

Stained

Stinging

Strawberry

Striped

Tanned (in more ways than one)

Taut

Tender

Tenderized

Tinged (a color)

Tinted

Troublesome

Welted

White

Wide

Wiggling

Reactions to Spanking

Build up reactions to spanking gradually. If your heroine howls and thrashes with the very first spank, where are you going to go from there? Keep in mind there are physical *and* emotional/mental reactions. Your spankee might cry, but is she in pain, ashamed, relieved, repentant, or angry? And don't forget the spanker. What is he experiencing? What does he feel for her? And what does he think of himself for having spanked her?

Physical Actions or Responses

Attempt to seduce

Bargain

Beg for forgiveness

Beg for it to stop

Blink back tears

Bite the spanker

Brace hands on the floor, against the wall

Bratting

Call names (insult the spanker)

Caress the spankee

Check for color

Chide the spankee, call her young lady, little girl, etc.

Clasp hands

Clench one's fists

Comfort the spankee

Count the spanks

Cover one's mouth

Cover one's ass

Cower

Cry (weep, sob, tear up)

Cuddle

Curse

Embrace, hug, hold

Fidget

Fight

Flail

Flee

Flinch

Fondle in a sexual way

Naughty Words for Nice Writers

Gasp

Grab or Grasp (bedcovers, clothing)

Grimace

Grit one's teeth

Get sexually aroused

Get caught in one's clothing

Go limp

Glower, glare

Hide from the spanker

Hold one's breath

Hold the spankee's hands behind her/his back

Hold spankee by the waist

Howl

Inhale, exhale

Jerk

Kick

Kiss

Lecture

Massage

Order spankee to hold a pose

Order spankee to keep hands out of the way

Pound one's fists

Pout

Promise to obey, to reform

Relax

Resist

Restrain the spankee

Retreat

Roll (attempt to roll off spanker's lap)

Roll up one's sleeves

Rub

Run away

Scold

Scowl

Shake, shiver

Shout

Shudder

Shy away

Slap at the spanker

Squirm

Submit

Survey the redness

Tense

Test the redness (by pinching)

Naughty Words for Nice Writers

Thank the spanker for the spanking

Tremble

Tug on restraints

Twist away

Wail

Whimper

Wiggle

Wince

Wrestle

Writhe

Wiggle

Wipe tears

Emotional Reactions

These may change before, during and after the spanking — and the spanker and spankee will experience different emotions

Acceptance

Adoration

Agitation

Anger

Anxiety

Arousal

Calm

Comfort

Curiosity

Desire

Determination (to not be disciplined again, or to punish, or endure the spanking)

Disappointment

Disdain

Dislike

Distrust

Dizziness

Embarrassment

Empathy

Euphoria

Fear

Frustration

Guilt

Groundedness

Hate

Naughty Words for Nice Writers

Humiliation

Hurt (feelings)

Lightheadedness

Love

Lust

Nervousness

Outrage

Pride

Protective

Relief

Remorse

Resentment

Resignation

Respect

Satisfaction

Security

Shame

Shock

Sympathy

Tenderness

Trust

Uncertainty

Tip: First figure out what your character is feeling then decide how you *show* it with physical reactions, thoughts, and dialog.

Spanking Aftercare

A spanking scene doesn't end with the last swat. Following a spanking, it is customary for the top to provide for the comfort of the bottom (bottom meaning person, not ass, although that, too).

Apply soothing lotion

Assure spankee all is forgiven

Bathe spankee

Calm spankee

Cover, ensure spankee is warm

Cuddle on lap

Embrace/hug

Engage in anal intercourse

Engage in sexual intercourse

Kiss

Kiss the redness, welts

Rub buttocks

Say I love you

Threaten to spank again if the situation calls for it

(okay, not very comforting)

Tuck into bed

Vow to protect

Whisper soothing words

Spanking Implements

An implement is an object used to spank. It can be made specifically for spanking, like a paddle or a flogger, or it can be a "pervertible," an object originally intended for another purpose, such as a paint stirrer or a bath brush.

Bath brush

Belt

Birch rod, switch

Bundle of switches

Cane

Cutting board

Flogger – Strips of leather (or vinyl) attached to a solid handle.

Fly swatter

Hair brush

Hand

Loopy Johnny – looped cords attached to a handle. Not for beginners!

Paddle – wood, leather, leather-covered

Paint stirrer

Ping-pong paddle

Pervertible (non-spanking object used to spank with)

Riding crop

Rod

Rolled up newspaper or magazine

Rug beater

Ruler

Slipper, flip-flop

Spatula

Strap – like a belt, only it's already looped

Switch, tree branch

Tawse – Looks like belt, only made of stiffer leather and one end is split into tails (often 2, but it varies).

Wand (from mini blinds)

Whip

Wooden spoon

Items in a BDSM Dungeon

This entry sounds like a question on the Family Feud (if it were X-rated). "Top answers are on the board, name something you might find at a BDSM dungeon."

Blindfolds

Bondage bed

Butt plugs

Cage

Canes

Chastity belts

Cock ring

Crops

Condoms

Floggers

Gags

Handcuffs

Lube

Massage tables

Nipple clamps

Paddles

Restraints

Ropes

Saint Andrew's Cross

Spanking Bench

Spreader bar

Stocks

Suspension system

Violet wand

Wartenberg wheel

Wax

Spanking Positions

These are the basics. Variety can be added with the use of setting, toys, or props.

Over the knee (OTK)

Over his shoulder ("fireman's hold")

On one's hands and knees

Bent over an object (desk, sofa arm, table, etc.)

Grasping one's ankles

Lying on the bed

Naughty Words for Nice Writers

Facing, braced against a wall

Standing

Diaper position

Crouched on/over a spanking bench

Holding onto a bedpost

Over the Knee Verbs

You must decide whether the taken-in-hand willingly places her/himself over the spanker's knee or whether the spanker takes charge of that aspect. One can place oneself across another's knee—or *be* placed over a lap

Crawl

Drag

Drape

Ease

Fall

Fling

Flop

Haul

Lie

Lower

Place

Position

Pull

Recline

Settle

Naughty Words for Nice Writers

Shift

Squirm

Stretch out

Throw

Wiggle

Non-Spanking Punishments

These may be used instead of a spanking or in conjunction with one. Many of these scenarios edge into BDSM, but you'll still see them in spanking romances and domestic discipline stories.

Age play scenarios, treating spankee like a child
Anal discipline (use of butt plugs, finger, etc.)
Anal sex
Bondage
Clamping nipples
Corner time
Clothing restriction, forcing the spankee to go naked
Embarrassing physical exams (medical play, pelvic exams, enemas)
Forcing spankee to expose genitals
Forcing the spankee to apologize
Ginger figging
Isolation (putting spankee alone to think about what she/he has done)

Naughty Words for Nice Writers

Making the spankee choose the implement, kiss the implement

Making spankee spank herself

Mouth soaping

Lecturing, scolding

Orgasm restriction or forced orgasm

Photographing the spanked bottom or making the sub/bottom send Dom/top photos

Put on public display (nudity, reddened bottom, etc.)

Restriction of privileges

Sexual intercourse

Use of creams to enhance burning sensation

Waiting (making spankee wait & worry)

Writing lines

Naughty Words to Avoid

Here are some words you should limit during writing or eliminate during revision. Use your writing software program's search/find function to highlight them, then delete them and/or rewrite the sentence. Your story will be stronger for it. I'll show you some before and after examples of rewriting.

Back, down, up. These words are often redundant.

Before: She leaned back against the tub.

After: She leaned against the tub.

Before: He sat down.

After: He sat.

Before: They climbed up the stairs to look up at the sky.

After: They climbed the stairs to look at the sky.

Begin/began. Often characters don't need *to begin* anything. Have them *do* it. Don't say they've begun something, unless you also show them ending it.

Before: He began to get worried they'd never have sex.

After: He worried they'd never have sex.

Characters' names. Search for your characters' names to highlight how many times they pop up. Names often are overused. If it's obvious who is speaking or acting, consider deleting the name and/or rewriting the sentence. But remind readers of the names of the characters in the scene at least once per scene.

Even. Delete most references.

Feel/felt. Show the emotion, don't state it.

Before: Her hurt glances made him feel even worse

After: Her hurt glances jabbed at his conscience.

Just. Delete most usages of this word.

Knew/know. Eliminating know and knew will deepen the point of view.

Before: Marcie knew a relationship between them would never work.

After: A relationship between them would never work.

Look. Characters do too much "looking" because authors use this verb as a dialog tag. Substitute a more creative action.

Before: She looked at John. "You intend to spank me?"

After: She clutched her necklace. "You intend to spank me?"

L-Y words. Words ending in "ly" are adverbs that tell about the action. Delete them, and substitute a stronger verb to carry the load.

Before: He walked quickly into the sex club.

After: He hurried into the sex club.

A search for ly words will catch totally, really, and only, which are overused. Delete most of those.

Made/make. Rewriting these words out of a sentence strengthens it. Same thing with cause/caused.

Not. Not turns a positive into a negative, but using a single word that means the same thing will be more descriptive. Most nots will be hidden in contractions: didn't, don't, won't.

Before: She didn't want to run into him.

After: She avoided him.

Before. "I don't like you!"

After: "I hate you!"

Smile. Similar to look, smile gets used too often as a dialog tag.

That. Delete as many as you can.

Took/take. Similar to made/make. Using another word will enliven your writing.

Turn. Eliminate and/ or substitute a synonym. Writers overuse turn for two reasons. First, they use it as a dialog tag. *Mandy turned to Roger. "You want to tie me up and have your wicked way with me?"* Second, they use it to convey motion. *She turned and flounced from the room.* She can pivot or spin. But why does she need to turn/spin/rotate at all? Why not, she flounced away?

Think/thought. If you eliminate usage in dialog, you will focus more on the message:

Before: I think we should kidnap him and ransom him for a billion dollars.

After: Let's kidnap him and ransom him for a billion dollars.

There's nothing wrong with the first example, and in real life, people say, "I think" all the time. But you're not writing about real life, you're writing fiction and it should be better and more exciting than real.

Also, eliminating thought and think from narration will deepen the point of view. It transforms telling into showing. Don't inform the reader your character is thinking of something, just have your character think it.

Before: Mandy thought the guy in Accounting was really cute, but he'd never go for her. She slumped and stirred her coffee.

After: *That guy is Accounting is so cute. He'd never go for me*. She slumped and stirred her coffee.

Try/tried. Like begin/began, try/tried is often unnecessary. Try connotes an attempt that did not pan out. Ask yourself if that accurately describes the scenario.

Use. Characters "use" a lot of items. Find a more descriptive verb.

Before: He used a paddle to swat her ass.

After: He swatted her ass with a paddle. Or: He paddled her ass.

Before: He used a pen to write down her phone number.

After: He jotted down her phone number.

Walk. Walk is so neutral it almost begs for an ly adverb, so find another verb to convey the tone. Your character can creep, inch, stride, skip, stomp, wander, flounce, sashay. See the difference?

Very. Very is an adverb without the "ly" warning label. Eliminate it and/or strengthen the adjective to which it is attached.

Before: I'm very tired.

After: I'm exhausted.

Was. The BIG bugaboo. *If you do nothing else*, limiting *was* in your manuscript will improve your writing by forcing you to use active voice and select stronger verbs. I've read excellent books in which the authors used quite a few *wases*, but they were exceptions. Use *was* for a reason, when the sentence needs it, not as a fallback or out of laziness.

In romance, was gets used a lot to describe a character's appearance. *Her hair was auburn*. But how about, *her auburn hair blazed under the lights*. Or, *Her auburn hair caught the light and his attention*.

So how many *wases* are too many? Rule of thumb: Allow yourself an average of three per page. So a 200-page manuscript would have 600. Does that mean you can't have a page with five *wases*? No. It's an average.

But if you see a paragraph with five *was* sentences, give it a second look.

Want. Want is overused in romance as a synonym for desire. But now that you have this thesaurus, you can substitute a more concise, descriptive term.

Final tip: Also search for words specific to your story and your favorite catch phrases. Chances are you're using them too much.

About the Author

USA Today Bestselling Author Cara Bristol has written more than fifty romance titles. She got her start in publishing by writing erotic romance (spanking romance) for Loose Id, Decadent Publishing, Blushing Books, and Black Velvet Seductions before going Indie and switching to science fiction romance. As of this writing, she has six sci-fi romance series: Alien Mate, Breeder, Dakonian Alien Mail Order Brides, Alien Dragon Shifters, Alien Castaways, and the Men of Mettle Cyborg Romance series. She holds a B.A. in journalism but also took several human sexuality classes in college because she thought they would be easy As. (Two were, one wasn't). Married with two grown step kids, Cara lives in the sunny, but conservative, state of Missouri where people often look askance when she tells them what she does for a living. You can visit Cara on her website/blog at https://www.carabristol.com. Subscribe to her newsletter (http://eepurl.com/9aRJj) and get a free book. (You can read her sex scenes!).

Titles by Cara Bristol

Alien Mate series

Alien Mate (Book 1)

Alien Attraction (Book 2)

Alien Intention (Book 3)

Alien Mischief (Book 4)

Alien Mate Complete Series Boxed Set

Dakonian Alien Mail-Order Brides
(Intergalactic Dating Agency)

Darak

Aton

Caid

Sixx

Kord

Braxx

Dakonian Alien Mail Order Brides Box Set Vol 1

Dakonian Alien Mail Order Brides Box Set Vol. 2

Alien Castaways

(Intergalactic Dating Agency)

Chameleon

Wingman

Psy

Men of Mettle series

Cyborg Protector (Book1)

Cyborg Husband (Book 1.5)

Cyborg Rogue (Book 2)

Cyborg Boss (Book 3)

Cyborg Heat (Book 4)

Cyborg Mate (Book 5)

Cyborg Rescuer (Book 6)

Cyborg Commander (Book 7)

Men of Mettle Cyborg Romance Collection

Breeder sci-fi romance series

Breeder (Book 1)

Terran (Book 2)

Warrior (Book 3)

Naughty Words for Nice Writers

Alien Dragon Shifters

Under Fyre

Line of Fyre

Other titles

Destiny's Chance

Warrior's Curse

Longing, a vampire romance

Naughty Words for Nice Writers (A Romance Novel Thesaurus)

You're Not Ugly To Look At

Spanking Romance Titles

Rod and Cane Society Series

Unexpected Consequences

False Pretenses

Body Politics

Disciplinary Measures

Reasonable Doubts

Irresistible Attractions

Audiobooks

Stranded with the Cyborg

Mated with the Cyborg

Books in Print

Alien Mate

Captured by the Cyborg

Claimed by the Cyborg

Naughty Words for Nice Writers

You're Not Ugly To Look At

Acknowledgements

I owe a special thank you to author Celeste Jones who suggested the title, *Naughty Words for Nice Writers*, because otherwise, I might have just called it, Sex Scene Thesaurus, or something equally boring. Graphics whiz Jaycee DeLorenzo of Sweet 'N Spicy Designs did the cover. As you know from reading the intro, this is the third iteration of Naughty Words, but I've kept the same cover with every revision. You can't improve on awesome! I also am indebted to my original beta readers Celeste, Maren Smith, Sue Lyndon, Natasha Knight, and Alison Aimes. Last, but not least, I thank editor Kate Richards of Wizards in Publishing for her hawk eyes and red pen.